I AM THE MOST DANGEROUS THING

I AM THE MOST DANGEROUS THING

POEMS

CANDACE WILLIAMS

Alice James Books
NEW GLOUCESTER, MAINE
alicejamesbooks.org

CELEBRATING 50 YEARS OF ALICE JAMES BOOKS

10 9 8 7 6 5 4 3 2 1

Alice James Books are published by Alice James Poetry Cooperative, Inc.

Alice James Books
Auburn Hall
60 Pineland Drive, Suite 206
New Gloucester, ME 04260
www.alicejamesbooks.org

Library of Congress Cataloging-in-Publication Data

Names: Williams, Candace (Poet), author.
Title: I am the most dangerous thing : poems / Candace Williams.
Description: New Gloucester, ME : Alice James Books, [2023]
Identifiers: LCCN 2022049495 (print) | LCCN 2022049496 (ebook) | ISBN
    9781949944525 (trade paperback) | ISBN 9781949944259 (epub)
Subjects: LCGFT: Poetry.
Classification: LCC PS3623.I56726 I25 2023 (print) | LCC PS3623.I56726
    (ebook) | DDC 811/.6--dc23/eng/20221125
LC record available at https://lccn.loc.gov/2022049495
LC ebook record available at https://lccn.loc.gov/2022049496

Alice James Books gratefully acknowledges support from individual donors, private foundations, the National Endowment for the Arts, and the Amazon Literary Partnership.

Cover art: "Untitled II", 2020, M. Florine Démosthène. Cover pattern: djero.adlibeshe yahoo.com. Interior pattern: Ineke Lablaika.

CONTENTS

I AM THE MOST DANGEROUS THING

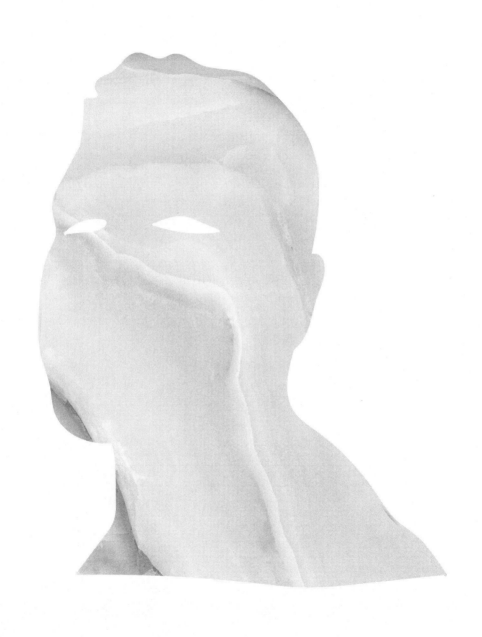

THIS BOOK IS THE PROPERTY OF:

Eyes pick apart my cornrows
as our teacher recites: *Slavery*
in the Americas from a textbook **ISSUED:NEW** that day   (Social Studies)

Our tiny hands paste cotton balls to thick blue
paper constructing fields
from text-heavy descriptions of the **CONDITION:USED**   (Art)

We copy   **STATE**   **COUNTY**   **SCHOOL DISTRICT**
from the whiteboard to the bookplate
Pride curls my tongue to upper lip   (Penmanship)

We were captured
and now I'm surrounded by white
kids highlighting

dense passages
in silence: *Supreme*
defy

Dred Scott
denied
CHAPTER QUIZ tomorrow   (Comprehension)

MORALS OF WORK

MOMMA SAID

For Ellen Williams and Arhonda Reyes

Momma said wake up.
Momma said it's time to get ready.
Momma said you'll be late.
Momma said your clothes are in the dryer.
Momma said get up.
Momma said get ready.
Momma said put your clothes on.
Momma said put your clothes on right now.
Momma said NOW.
Momma said your hair is a mess.
Momma said you should wear a headscarf to bed.
Momma said bring her a comb and some grease.
Momma said you need a new relaxer.
Momma said wash the sleep out of your eyes.
Momma said take the chicken out of the freezer.
Momma said don't forget again.
Momma said don't forget lunch.
Momma said don't forget your gym shorts.
Momma said don't forget she'll be home late.
Momma said don't forget your keys.
Momma said don't forget your coat.
Momma said she doesn't work this hard for you
to be cold.
Momma said don't forget yourself.
Momma said you forgot the chicken last week
and if she has to go to Popeyes again, you aren't getting any.
Momma said wait until the car warms up.
Momma said find good music.
Momma said she'll never understand people who listen to prank calls on the way to work.
Momma said she'll take Gladys Knight over Babyface any day of the week.
Momma said you look exhausted.
Momma said your math teacher humiliates you on purpose.
Momma said keep your head down and your pencil up.

Momma said we work twice as hard.

Momma said she works late to save for private school.

Momma said you'll get in.

Momma said you'll get in.

Momma said you can't walk into school crying.

Momma said take a deep breath.

Momma said blow your nose.

Momma said there are tissues in the glove compartment.

Momma said you can't be everything at everything.

Momma said you'll be there in two minutes.

Momma said summer is almost here.

Momma said you'll sleep in.

Momma said you should splash water on your face before you go to class.

Momma said we're here.

PRINCIPLES OF VALUE

The first step to finding self-
worth is breaking yourself
into units

of desire: gender is a binary
defined by genitals
academic degrees mark wisdom

your skin's degree
of pigment
proxies ancestry—your

ancestors were naturally rich
in melanin
your ancestors

were tallied
on shopping lists
your ancestors

were the squeezed
and haggled fruits
at a market

stand, but you never left
the market—the market
is your bedroom

the market is last
night's dream
the market

is your love
sleeping next to you
is your buzzing

alarm you wake up
in a panic searching
for an exit

smoke obscures
your vision: gender
seems binary

because expression is taxed
to the margin
academic degrees

are mistaken for wisdom
because privilege is a discount
on prosperity

your skin's degree
of pigment taxes
the nerves of privilege

your skin's degree
of pigment
is the weight

of every sunk ship
in the Atlantic
your skin's degree

of pigment
is the flowering
soil of progress

THE DARK DIARY

The day was ending   in stained light
the west glowing   white without rays
without heat: sudden   death by touch
of brooding men a   change came over
the water   we looked vivid
in august   light
as the phrase   goes: *terror*   *knows ships bear*
the sword   this stir of light
is lurid glare   there is nothing
mysterious—hours   of work
a casual spree   a whole continent
the shell of a cracked nut   the glow brings
a haze: misty halo but   Darkness was here
Darkness, the colour   of kin
of order   white is a bundle
of cold tempests—exile   death: death
skulking the air   Darkness survived
the awful climate   the trader savagery
utter savagery   fascination—abomination   preaching
in european   clothes
efficiency...devotion   *to efficiency*
account administration   a squeeze
brute force   an accident
the conquest of the earth   a sacrifice
we understand the effect of   light on everything   a pitiful kind
of light invading   your homes
just a heavenly mission   to civilize
you: a white dream   vast country
a company—fresh departure   I wouldn't have
believed   myself but Black
is asserting   self-respect in some
way   the white man   expects all
kinds of opportunity: grass   growing tall enough
to hide   the bones—they

were all there   Black men

children the cause   of progress: whited

sepulchre   we were going to

run through   vast white

its light a heavy pale   I found myself   again: I am young

and Black   walking back

and forth   guarding the door   of Darkness knitting

black wool for the young   and the dead

I said *yes*   produced a thing   I have a little

theory: my country   shall reap

from my possession   my observation   was not typical

I was also one   of the workers

light is such rot   I ventured queer

feeling came to me   I was an imposter:

almost Black fringed   white ran

straight like   a ruled line

sun whitish   with the idleness

of a passenger   my isolation

seemed to keep me   from the truth

of things: mournful   senseless delusion

a momentary contact   with reality

you could see from   afar—white bodies

faces grotesque masks   intense energy

an excuse   for being   there I saw

the mouth   speaking english

with great precision   and considerable

bitterness I   wonder: what   becomes god?

a reach?   a waste?

continuous noise   sunlight drowned

all this   I came back   Black on the face

of a rock Black   in file balancing

time Black   force at work

seeing white on the path   white men being

so much (and not   particularly tender)

I've had to strike   and to fend off

I've had to resist and attack   that's one way

of resisting   counting   the exact cost of life blundered into

the devil—a

the purpose of which

desire I discovered

against light

and despair

fed on unfamiliar food

the Black

of the orbs: Sister Phantom

I didn't want any

I made haste

Dark eternity

again

agent bent

transactions—the sound

country

at the end

that originate

it had been a door

Darkness

waiting

passing invasion

bursts into blaze

the glowdark

hissing ruin

the only real

a singleness of purpose

lots of them

I interrupt

of virtue

who sent light

opportunity

ascended moonlight's brute

telling the manager

discussing the mysterious

life—the hurt

the false idea

the noise stopped

a bell

various things

how insidious

vast artificial hole

is philanthropic

my purpose: Black

attitudes of pain

Black shadow

free as air

flicker in the depths

in every pose

more loitering

set off toward

I began to write

at the door: the

over books making

in a christian

white men retire

of speeches

nothing as though

opening into

surrounding truth

patiently for the

happen: cotton

I approach

I found myself

of government

feeling was desire

who says that?

some even write

the new gang: gang

the same people

to produce

the hissing

transgressions:

gesticulating

reality of concealed

the deep sigh

of disposition this

papier-mache
the wreck hauled
the smell primeval mud
about himself
strayed here
knows his fiend
I want to forget
and the rest
pilgrims
the story?
to tell you
commingling
bewilderment
struggling revolt
captured by the very essence
disturbed
pilgrims empty
charmed brutes
in the moonlight
a gutter
what it really means
purpose is a clattering
obscures
I did not know
why we shouldn't
a visitation in white
disorderly flight of loot
stores: they were lugging
equitable division
made the spoils
reckless
they seem aware
wanted—tearing
out the bowels
no moral purpose
into safe
in poor neighborhoods
worrying myself

mephistopheles poked in

you know I can't bear

every rifle

sleep

there came an invasion
instalments

cruel

about their morals

I did try to stop him
up on the shore
white man jabbered
a menace who
a confounded god
a lie
europe
of the bewitched
do you see
I am trying
a dream: a
of absurdity
a tremor of
a notion of being
of light glittering
the bad habit
they lay hands on
a charmed life
glittering empty
they never tell
I suppose white
my Dark figure
the lighted doorway
of any reason
an infliction
an absurd
of innumerable
a raid against
human folly
of thieving sordid
without courage
these things are
treasure
of their desire
burglars break
enterprise
I had given up
of work

MEMO:

Due to unforeseen circumstances
I am forced to lay off 20% of my friends
effective immediately.

A climate of deteriorating privilege
means I must tighten the alignment between emotional labor
and future growth opportunities.

Change is difficult;
these decisions are not made lightly.

Those affected will receive
severance tied
to years of kinship.

I appreciate the civility and support of the team
as I secure our long-term competitive advantage.

STATE TEST

I oversee rows of hands working to prove
their worth they bubble names on Scantron forms
so the state knows them without knowing them

answer questions about the texture of kitten fur
handle objects most adults can't name
they drop spheres into graduated cylinders

note the rise in meniscus or depth of water splashed:
this displacement *is volume* I walk between rows
of children uniformed in neon

shirts this displacement is volume; last month
my principal replaced our class pets with blue book exams
this is volume too—soon, trucks loaded with stacks

of chicken scratch will traverse the FDR screeching
toward a high-rise where white women wait
for cargo they hang coats on wires

and refuse foam cups of coffee they hate my kids
because they miss their own waking before the sun
to sum a fourth-grader's knowledge

of volume, mass and density density is mass
over volume also called compactness; my students
labor in an 8 x 4 rectangle

you can hear the frequent hiss of *sorrys*
when elbows knock this is mass over volume
a kid knocks over her cylinder the water and sphere

drop to the floor we overflow from this moment or
we're already forgotten in the deluge or
I'm a cylinder sent to contain too much of what is not myself.

THEOREM

For Julie Kraft

Suppose x loses 1:   This is $x - 1$ This is also $x + (-1)$

Loss also is an accumulation.

Let x be any human thing.

Suppose you break up with me.

This absence has a multitude of expressions.

Every night loses its kiss; every crisis its comfort.

And so on.

With each day of absence, a mass swells at your core.

Wine drowns the swelling—so you hope.

Now, consider the ache after you binge.

Hunger is a sign of depletion

so you take the first bite

and keep biting.

You're hurting.

You've consumed more than your body

can handle.

The pain worsens by the mouthful.

You eat to feed another

depleted mass you're afraid to name.

Empty states are real, burning things.

Recall being a kid alone in bed when your mother was somewhere else.

Remember how the weight of her absence burdened your chest to the mattress.

You breathe, air filling and escaping carved volumes.

Your breaths shallow as the swelling takes shape.

Your mother returns home; enters your dark room.

She kisses your forehead—each feather touch lifting something.

Her breaths become shallow too.

You know she wants to wake you

and doesn't want to wake you.

You pretend to sleep, leaving the lifting to her.

She carries the absence to bed.

DESK LUNCH POEM

I eat leftovers
at my desk
because being a Black
woman who can always be found
working is the only reason
they let me eat

JOHN HENRY SUFFERING AND DYING IN THE ARMS OF HIS POLLY ANN AFTER A VENTRICULAR RUPTURE RESULTING FROM OVERWORK

I drove through slag and ore so men could move
the Coosa Mountain, God not seen. I fought
and won and found no prize because this work
is not the will of God. The will of God
is not the greed of gluttons—masters who
are now the captains. Captain Dabney made
this bet—he told the salesman my sledge could beat
a drill that's pushed by steam and metal parts.
My sledge is forty pounds. I beat the machine.
Oh Captain! Captain? Pilot   oh   pilot   me...
I was his slave by birth. I lived and toiled
in bondage under Master Dabney now
I die from toil under Captain Dabney.
I'm blind, my Polly Ann. I'm blind...you rock
a dying man like mothers rock infants
who see the world with new, soft eyes. I'm blind!
I hear the roar of hammers striking stone
and know no hammer stops for me. I loved
my hammer more than thirsty men must love
a dip of water from a running stream.
I loved my hammer's sound—it rang through night.
It rang through rock. It kept the pace. I saw
it raised above my head and then I saw
no more. I worked to eat and worked to live.
The Captain lives to gain. The Captain lives.
His children live. His children ride the rail.
I swung my sledge. They ride the rail. I swung
my sledge. My Polly Ann! The Captain lives.

FRUIT

From this computer I uproot lush gardens—I'm paid to discover new fruit
Dutifully, I bow to profit, palm rich soil, pluck low-hanging fruit

When summer comes, I mouth the dripping stone fruit over my kitchen sink
Each bite a celebration—a glory of forgetting the blood sown to pick my abundance of fruit

I pray I'm not a mercenary fleeced by comfort; I crave a natural death for us all
If I am seeded in a bed of lemoned earth, will I burn for reaping soured fruit?

Trauma's deposits enlarge my dark frame: I'm a twinge of pinched nerves and strained arteries
White eyes behind the X-ray render my pain, ask, *Aren't you even trying to eat more fruit?*

Imagine Abel composing his famous pastoral—his *bitter crops*, my *blood on the leaves*
I spend dark hours sifting myself from white gaze: I invade the still life, smash the bowl of fruit

And how do you comfort young Candace, a poet exhausted and hurting from truth?
Call on her at tea and pour over Ali's ghazals while slicing into spring fruit

COMMUTE

For Jason Koo

I hop off the 5
at Bowling Green
and can't remember
if I turned off my stove burner
before I left
my apartment in Crown Heights

I remember rushing
to pour water
from the whistling kettle
waiting four minutes
for it to steep
over coarse grounds
I remember my front door slamming
but don't remember
turning the dead bolt
walking to President Street
or swiping my MetroCard

I remember giving up
my rush hour seat
to an older lady
in a tan trench coat
who looked down at me
like she didn't expect me
to rise for her
I remember watching her
realize her own disbelief
a moment after it hit her face
hearing a mumbled *Thank you*
as she slunk down to her seat

I don't remember Atlantic or Nevins
I remember remembering
I need to exercise more
passing Borough Hall
because my old gym is there
next to a Shake Shack
I remember the crisp colorful lunch
I'd rushed to pack
in stainless steel
while the kettle came to a boil
knowing I'd eat
a cheeseburger instead

I lose a breath tripping
over a loose stair
and look up
at the park
I'm surrounded
by chipper tourists
in bright Canada Goose parkas
lining up to pose
in front of the Charging Bull
sculpture
gripping its bronze balls
in their hands
while smiling
for smartphones

I see tourists
asking cops
to pose
for photos
see the cops
oblige with smiles
decide to wait
for the impromptu
NYPD photo shoot

to end
before passing
in front of the smiler
taking photos
I wish
my patience was a courtesy
to out-of-towners
or the art of photography
but I've learned to avoid the gaze
of cops
assigned to the morning shift

A power-walking man
in pinstripes
carrying a cup
of coffee gyrating over its edge
cuts through the scene
just before the iPhone flash
I tag behind him
the same way I often trail
white people crossing
busy intersections
against the light

CROWN HEIGHTS

She pulls the curtain back and light engulfs
her prewar home. The sun illuminates
the parquetry and lines of lacquered oak
around the walls. The kettle boils; she grinds
the coffee beans and weighs the grounds. She drinks
her coffee while she reads the *Times*. She puts
her pit bull into coat and boots. They do
their morning routine—heading west on Crown
to Rogers; turning right and buying sweets
near President; going east to Nostrand
and walking back to Crown. She walks the heart
of Crown Heights. She walks the ghost perimeter
of Crow Hill Castle—named after murders
of crows that flocked to trees atop the hill;
or darkies lined up on the hill like crows;
or the louring inmates dressed in crow black.
She's never heard of this Crow Hill;
the county tore it down and built Crown Heights.
The county built and ran the Castle too.
The walls were made of stone and pitched thirty
feet high. Eight turrets enclosed five acres.
Women were jailed with infants in their cells.
The men were forced to dig the city roads.
The women stitched; they sewed 15,000
leather shoes per day. The Sabbath sermon
rang from chapel under sobs and screams
of men and women whipped with frayed cowhide.
The inmates starved or had to eat the bad
food—rancid butter, rotted fish and meat.
She walks past a CrossFit gym named
Crow Hill and enters a coffee shop called
Colina Cuervo. She likes the croissants.

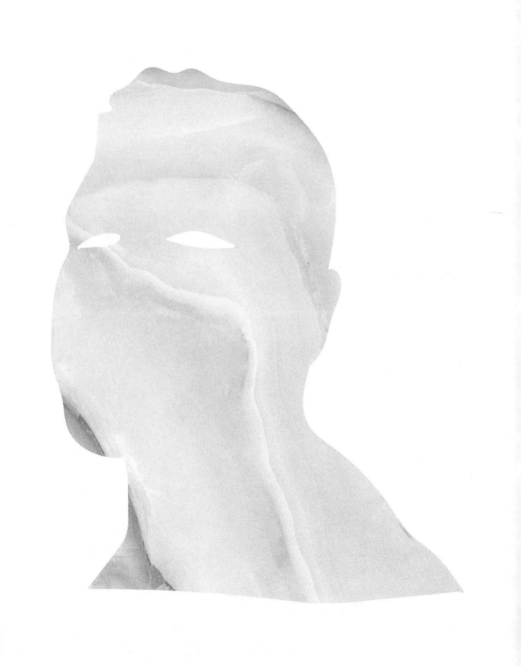

THE SHAPE OF A NOISY DREAM

WHEN I WAS 12

For Harold Williams

my dad told the psychiatrist I suffer

night terrors because I'm evading   generations   of trauma

the heritage of Middle Passage   was dismissed by science

so the psychiatrist dismissed dad's   evidence

nodding *mmhmmm*   I was prescribed

a bottle of Paxil

and I swallowed   my Paxil

daily   yet I suffered

nightly   the psychiatrist prescribed

more doses to stop   trauma

from animating my body while I slept   he stressed evidence

recorded in elite   journals of medicine and science

and years later ancestral trauma was re-created   in a science

lab   I flushed my Paxil

after reading the evidence

men in white coats   electrocuted mice until the animals suffered

convulsions at the scent of cherry blossoms   this scent traumatized

offspring who never experienced electric current   men in white coats prescribe

trauma to bury trauma   they'll excavate later   my psychiatrist prescribed

Paxil because he didn't know   why a 12-year-old   science

geek escaped her bed   screaming bloody murder in her sleep   *the trauma*

must stem from chemical imbalance   he said   *Paxil*

stimulates neurotransmitters   but he didn't know my suffering

is a transmission from the belly of *Desire* crossing the atlantic   there's evidence

my ancestral bodies survived   and did not survive   this ship   evidence

human cargo   was prescribed

bondage   and suffering

because states   need building   scientists

endorsed these prescriptions with eugenic theories   my Paxil

is evidence of trauma

inflicted by these white coats   who are paid   per trauma
          they gather   evidence
for cures by handing out placebos   *the Paxil*
is a placebo   I screamed   my psychiatrist prescribed
higher doses   and I became his science
experiment   white coats dissected my suffering

in labs resembling bedrooms   they prescribed
more Klonopin   more scans   more *mmhmmm*   more science
still screaming: *I suffer*

LADY

LADY

_____

Is

_____

_____

Seen   Only by

    negroes

        Every   night
    negroes assemble to watch for
the

                        visitor

        lady

                    is

        dark and
    howling

29

white

       hanging down her back,
she

                         demanded,
"Me chee-ild. where is me chee-ild?"

                            every
night. asking for her lost child
       the police

                    began telling
the neighbors

don't believe the

                      female

   The   neighbors turned   a
shade paler and
                  there was a deep
    oppressive silence

BOP FOR THE BOYS SCRIMMAGING IN PROSPECT PARK

For Gary Williams

On Sunday mornings, helmets cradle heads
of Black boys
who drill tackling
from the hip
They stand in a circle
waiting for their names

Stay in   the field   O warrior!
Stay in the field   until the war   has ended

The boy in the middle can't leave
until he's taken a hit
from each 8 year old
Coach calls him punk
if his body clears the pit
Coach says meaner things
if his little Hawks hesitate or hold back
The boy in the middle grits his mouthguard

Stay in   the field   O warrior!
Stay in the field   until the war   has ended

Onlookers cheer each crunch
of collision: the clatter of polycarbonate protecting
fledgling bones and organs
The team peels off white
jerseys while the boy in the middle brags
the fresh bruises on his chest

Stay in   the field   O warrior!
Stay in the field   until the war   has ended

BOP FOR A BLACK MAN CAGED IN THE CONGO AND THE BRONX

One Pygmy patriarch or chief. One adult woman, preferably his wife.
Two infants. A priestess. A priest. The President
of the National Geographic Society pens a wish
list of human exhibits for the World's Fair
He admires two Batetela boys
offered to the Smithsonian

I believe	I'll go back	home
Lordy	won't you help	me?

A missionary leaves New York Harbor for the mouth
of the Congo; he carries eighty cases of black powder to hunt
the healthy among Mbuti peoples
mutilated by Leopold's slavers
In Bassongo, the Christian captures a soul
christens him Otabenga on the ship's manifest
The press calls him *Strange Little African, Artiba, Autobank, Ota Bang*

I believe	I'll go back	home
Lordy	won't you help	me?

40,000 New Yorkers mob the Monkey House
each day; they jeer the khaki-suited man
around the Bronx Zoo's walled gardens and the chambers of the American
Museum of Natural History; ten years later in Lynchburg
before he fires a bullet through his own heart
Baptist brothers hear their dear *Otto* sing:

I believe	I'll go back	home
Lordy	won't you help	me?

EXPLORER

Brings

ica   .to Amer-
                                           All
    things he has taken
         He

       worked with great speed, tying
strings   His haste was
due to his desire

           He is most expert in
         the ability to make snares
        one of the necessary accom-
plishments of his people. His nimble fin-
gers   make a net, with great rapid-
ity   These nets

           are stretched
   great distances
            and   drive
    prey into the snares, where they
             become en-
tangled.

            His favorite play-
ground is

            Africa
so many deities convenient for his vener-
ation.

                                        clad in
   a kaki jacket
                              He
   grins   good-naturedly and says
   " Yes " to all questions
   one of the very few   words he
   knows.

              he has seen so many
       things'
              he is beyond feeling

       white man began in a   ship.

       silent   showing
   the whites of his eyes and
   teeth

NOSTRAND AVENUE DIRGE

For Denise Bell

I am a makeshift procession crunching
down honey-leafed streets—
an acolyte to the forgotten bones whispering
under grumbling 2 trains, men
on the corner begging for smiles
and offbeat bars of "Could You Be Loved" rattling
car windows.
I pray my solemn alchemies transform
steaming coffee to thurible
and lambswool to cassock
but I cannot bear
witness for ancestors whose griots were massacred
and ink deemed criminal.
I dwell
upon their broken vertebrae and mouth
a gentle tribute.

QUANTA

The delicate ridge swelling around your rest
reminds me that you are not sleep, sunlight, bed, or blanket
You begin
and end sticking out of the covers
This is the simplest dimension
Another being the depth
of hollows that remain in your wake
The volume of held breath estimates the magnitude of depressions
Hot breaths, wet curls, and cold toes have
become my notes and hours

Although precision is the aim
of certainty, I alter what I measure
If I find out where you are going
I delay your departure
To keep your pace
is to displace you
This is the paradox of wanting
and wanting to know—
even in repose, we waver
between embrace and constraint

AFTER THE RAIN

beads down   Nostrand's windows   I count the blues
Ephemeral shades of storm's wake   an eye shined navy   an oil slick's iridescent blues

I stared at a psychiatrist's off-white   walls   once a week   after school
He prescribed baby   doses of Paxil   I imagined swallowing   the sea   of blue

After the rain   Nostrand's awnings   are emptying harbors
Folks pretend   they're on their way to   somewhere to   avoid the boys   in blue

Dad used to drive me   to the white   music teacher   across town
She thwacked my fingers   to frets   I still   remember   the chords of her   blues

After the rain Nostrand Av   is heavy with the funk of petrichor   fighting petroleum's fumes
Black children zigzag   the clinic line   coughing up flecked mucus   as their little faces blue

Mom says I was never a child never   a belly laugh or   smiling eyes
From night's door   she'd sigh   *Why is Candace so*   *so blue?*

THE DARK DIARY

It did not occur to me: I was sleeping
I had rather be alone than have the kind of men

you imagine: an invoice the reply fired out
then silence lying perfectly I'd intended

to return after coming suddenly decided
to go back I seemed to see for the first time:

the lone white man turning his back setting face
toward a desolate station: work for its own sake

the manager was saying *we will not be free* *from competition*
europe *a beacon: humanizing...* *improving...*

instructing... that ass his sunlit face
a treacherous appeal to lurking death unhidden evil

so startling I had to answer— a Black display
of confidence high stillness ominous patience

waiting for the passing invasion they pretend
not to know anything of my existence the sun tugging

painfully bending a single blade I know the fate
of the rest of us there is no joy in the brilliance

of sunshine gloom and silver sun side by side
you lost your way yourself bewitched and cut off

one's past came back to one in the shape
of a noisy dream overwhelming realities: a strange silence

force brooding I had no time I was learning
heart had to keep a lookout for signs

of the dead   you have to attend to surface   realities
be civil growled a voice   I was awake   beside myself

white men had the appearance   of being   there—a spell
reaches   between high walls   reverberating

in hollow claps   I imagined Darkness   it was very quiet
there—a night   of peace and prayer   stillness burned low

we cursed the cost   of excessive toil   sudden Black—
Black phantom   we remember   travelling

in the night   of our first memories   earth seemed
unearthly   we are accustomed   to freedom

it would come slowly   what thrilled you   was the thought
of kinship   the faintest   trace of response

joy   devotion   rage
truth stripped of acquisition   a deliberate belief   an appeal

I have a voice   that cannot be   silenced
between whiles   I had to look   for the queer

patterns: witchcraft   full knowledge   transparent thirst
this was unexpected   I found faded pencil-writing   when deciphered

it was illegible—it said   a much longer word   for warning
I picked up the book   lovingly stitched   with white thread

its title: *An Inquiry*   *into Matters*   a dreary read
diagrams   repulsive figures   the breaking strain

of chains   a singleness of intention   an honest concern
for the right   way of going to work   luminous chains

and purchases   pilgrims in delicious   sensation
this miserable trader   this intruder   I trouble darkly

observe assumed innocence
the wretched

the last flicker of human
my silence

what anyone knew
my power

I must approach daylight
expression

the lightest sleep
you began to suspect

a shutter
from all sides: *what*

Black dignity
is proper soul

the corpses
by many dangers sleeping

attack filled those savages
seen the pilgrims

choking stifling
I saw a man's

the middle passage
uninterrupted shoal

supported by Black
I swore

saw vague
I had been striving

I caught myself listening
to give up

patience
any action of mine

or ignored?
I judged my grave: the sun

no Dark hours
in the middle

an unnatural state
yourself

a towering multitude
is meaning?

what you may
a kind of scruple

in a battlefield
in fabulous castles

with unrestrained apathy
they delivered a regular

aggressive
backbone

it was much narrower
overgrown ranks

furnace the pilgrims
I wouldn't lose

forms of evanescent men
without substance

expected
it was like watching

my speech
what did it matter

a flash beyond
being very low

reach beyond
a narrow high sun

of trance
of being a gun fired

the sun screams
Black phrases

call Black
amongst

I was beset
the thought of

you should have
lecture: cotton-

in the unusual sense
running down

than I supposed
of rigid light

open fire
I threw my head

to tell you the truth
I couldn't have been

more disgusted / I had travelled / all this way
for the sole purpose / of imagined discourse / the man

a voice / tones of jealous admiration / he collected
swindled / stolen all of his gifts / the one that stood

out was the gift / of expression: most / contemptible light
a deceitful flow / from the heart / how many powers

of Darkness / claimed for their own? / Darkness obscured
by back-breaking business / I am not trying to explain / I am trying

to account / for myself / I must suppress
the savage custom / of eloquence / beautiful light

strikes me now / as ominous / the argument
that white / must necessarily appear / we approach

them with benevolence / noble burning words / a magic phrase
a kind of note / at the foot of the last / page scrawled

in unsteady hand / figurative speaking: the dead / frighten souls
bitter the self / I am not prepared / to exact worth

of life we lost / I regret memory / a tree swayed
the wind heavy / heavy / heavier

I imagine the dead / a hopeless funeral / suddenly
I got it / interrupted / the light

heart / cut off / everybody
kissed / off restraint: pursued / a rage

I AM THE MOST DANGEROUS THING

BLACK SONNET

A Black child lies in blood and I'm still Black.
I scan news on my phone and I'm still Black.
They call my name to board and I'm still Black.
I sit and sip a Sprite and I'm still Black.
We take off right on time and I'm still Black.
I peer at vast blue sea and I'm still Black.
I take my black tea black and I'm still Black.
I read a piece by Marx and I'm still Black.
I get lost and turn back and I'm still Black.
I make the right slight right and I'm still Black.
I ring the front bell twice and I'm still Black.
My love smiles with her eyes and I'm still Black.
We kick it for a bit and I'm still Black.
I turn off all the lights and I'm still Black.

IN KINGDOM HALL

I spent my Sundays hating God and men.
The women dressed in cream or white to flaunt
their modesty. The floor was a monochrome rainbow
of heels—they must've ordered the patent
leather pumps in bulk from Sears. Women
could perform skits on stage and pass the mic
but could not take the podium. The men—
in whom the God of glory stashes all
the power that is not in heaven, all
the longing that is not of Satan's sway,
and all the wisdom that is not above
their heads—were draped in gray and black.
The congregation prayed, opened ocher books, and flipped
to a melody approved by the Society.
Marches like "We Are Jehovah's Army!"
and "Guard Your Heart" blared from a worn cassette.
The elders filled ninety minutes with lecture
while children raced to find every verse.
The flap of Bible pages pleased their parents—proof
they might return to Paradise on Earth. The parents
threatened kids with the End of Days—the pale
horseman named Death and Seven-Headed Beast
bring woe to wicked souls who argue, run
indoors, and talk during service, instead
of proving their parents' grasp of eternity.
I dressed in Sunday morning's darkest hours
so God would keep my mom on his eternal scroll.
I thumbed the pages and memorized the word of God.
I traced the death and slaughter sketched
on colorful *Watchtower* pages, knowing I would
not survive the Last Judgment. I yearned for my
mom's survival. I sang the songs. I clapped.

ON NEOLIBERALISM OR: WHY MY BLACK ASS IS TIRED

The only reason why I wake
up put on
a shirt put on
pants put on different
pants look in
the mirror buy myself
a coffee a sub-
way swipe a diet
Coke™ & a pack of peanut butter M&M's™
is because I can't eat
drink ride or stand
sit or lay my body down
(in my bed in my girlfriend's bed on a spring green
on a gynecologist's table or anywhere else)
unless my boss likes my outfit my manners &
my manner of speech & my taper
fade & my electric blue Cole Haan's™ & my light cardigan & my button-
down & my Stanford™ degree & my spread-
sheets & anything else I
bring to the office promptly
at 10 am & leave unsaid & locked
behind my apartment door when it slams at 8
:40 & I've already run down
half a flight of stairs & soon I'll pass 2 white™
bros in the lobby who seem
angry to see
me they never open
their door for me they eye me through
the peephole & apologize through
the door before turning
their Ed Sheeran™ down
at midnight before turning
it back up again at 2 before I say
Fuck it & drown

2 fingers of scotch at 3
& I'm steps behind the white™
bros leaving the building
& the front door slams as I reach
it & a Black man beyond
the door leers at me seems
angry at me it's not my fault I didn't say hello
last week I didn't recognize him
making his way through the dark
I never recognize myself
or my silence like that one
time a white™ coworker made
a joke that I labored in
the office like I was picking
cotton in the field & my boss likes his labor™ more
than he hates racists so here
we are riding the elevator to-
gether in silence like
that one time I woke on a spring green with
a concussion & no memories & the police™
officer seemed angry
I made a sound

THE POWERPOINT SLIDE SAYS WHITE PEOPLE HAVE RACIAL ANXIETY BECAUSE THEY WANT TO BE LIKED BY BLACK PEOPLE

Well I'm Black
& I like you
I really like you
I'll always sit
next to you at lunch
& laugh a belly laugh
to prove I'm with you
right next to you never
above you never
over your head
behind your back
beyond your reaching
never out of range out
of earshot   **you**
know
I don't know
you but I know your need
is greater than my need
my greatest need is work
meaning if you don't like me sitting
at this computer
then I will run
out of money & become
what nonprofits call *needy*
also meaning broke also
somehow meaning: deserving
downtrodden
down-and-out
I dwell on this when we disagree
in cubicles I   **worry**
my Black ass will end
up in the cold
so in this cube I'll imagine

the frigid wind wearing
my skin to bone
& I'll hold my fire
inside   **I'll remember**
my whitest therapist
praising   **my *distress***
tolerance he loved my ability
to reduce myself
to ash while insulating
your virgin lungs
from the char of my kindling
flesh I'll keep smiling & nodding
so you won't starve
me to death
& you'll giggle over
your deep sense
of embarrassment don't worry I know
deep down all you want:
is for me
all you want
is for me
all you want
is for me
all you want
is for me
all you want
is for me to like you
& I know you
don't mean it oh I know
your heart & being a woman
in the workplace is hard
in times like these & I know you
must be tired & race is tricky
sometimes & yes I know   **your great grandparents**
were immigrants from Scotland & they   **owned**
a farm & they also had
a hard time at first

& don't worry the boss
won't delay your promotion
to make room for   **Black**
candidates & yes other   **people**
might think that sounds racist
but don't worry   **I can imagine why**
                                                you're so nervous

so you don't need
to worry please
don't be anxious: I swear
I'm Black & I like you.

blackbody

"An ideal body is now defined, called a *blackbody...the blackbody is a perfect absorber...*"
—Robert Siegel and John R. Howell, *Thermal Radiation Heat Transfer*

A body can be perfectly black meaning it absorbs all radiance—all heat and light waves that fall upon it. A blackbody is perfect because it is a perfect absorber—all waves that strike its surface pass into the body and the body absorbs them internally. Nothing striking the blackbody passes through the body's edge. Nothing striking the blackbody is reflected back into the environment. The blackbody is perfect. It is opaque. It is not defined by its size or shape. It might not be black at all. The color black absorbs all wavelengths of light that fall upon it. The blackbody is named for its presumed blackness to the naked eye but a blackbody can be red or blue or another color. The blackness is theoretical. The blackbody is theoretical—a device used to give body to abstractions. Perfect black is a theoretical ideal—it has not been observed but exists for the sake of comparison. For the sake of comparison, the opposite of a blackbody is a white body. A white body reflects all waves perfectly in all directions. The albedo scale compares white bodies and blackbodies. Albedo comes from Arabic's *albayad*. *Albayad* roughly translates to "whiteness." Albedo is a measure of reflectivity and brightness. Scientists say the albedo effect is warming our planet beyond safety. Said another way, the whiteness effect is warming our planet beyond safety. 91% of Fortune 500 CEOs are white men. Outdoor air pollution has risen 8% in the past five years. The arctic is melting—the white ice is falling into the dark sea turning reflective surfaces into heat absorbers. It's getting warmer. By "it's getting warmer," I mean that in 2010, 10,000 scorched to death in Moscow. By "it's getting warmer," I mean that it was 116° in Portland last summer. By "it's getting warmer," I mean that by 2080, 3,300 will scorch to death each year on New York City streets, and half of those buried will be Black. It's getting warmer and I wonder about white men in boardrooms. I wonder about the PowerPoint presentations and profit diagrams. On the diagram, the blue line is profit. The Black bodies pile under the blue line over the axis of time and the blue line rises. In the boardroom, the Black body is the ideal— we absorb perfectly.

MY FUTURE/BLACK CERTIFICATE OF DEATH

32. PART I: CAUSE OF DEATH—My heart is 50% more / likely to fail / than a white woman's / chances are doctors will fail / to resuscitate me / & the doctor will state / my time of death & write superficial / causes / so I leave this / for you / to recite / when my time comes:

IMMEDIATE CAUSE (Final disease or condition ⟶ resulting in death)

walls of her
atria
ruptured

DUE TO

rapid constriction
cutting blood
flow

DUE TO

extra weight
carried
at her core

DUE TO

her overwhelming
desire to swallow it all
and her longing to lie down

DUE TO

the fact she could never stop
running and had been running
since before she was born

DUE TO

pounds
forced on her
ancestral bodies

DUE TO

pre-existing conditions and the deep
deep cuts that still
draw blood and still take cultures

DUE TO

hidden addiction: the dependency whites
have on **BLACK**
riches **BLACK** soil **BLACK**
brilliance **BLACK**
power **BLACK**
labor **BLACK**
rhythm **BLACK**
blues **BLACK**
country **BLACK**
rock **BLACK**
rap **BLACK**
art **BLACK**
cool **BLACK**
it's all **<u>BLACK</u>**
& you know it
& you never desired Candace's
freedom   Who desires **BLACK**
freedom?
                           Who desires **BLACK**
independence
                           when **BLACK** bodies are still
the nation's capital?

OWED

watching my mother balance   the family checkbook   seemed like the writing of odes:

some on-sale bananas   that dress   your bike laid away   there was always something owed

my senior english teacher assigned neruda   told me he was the world's passion: he sings to socks

praises tomatoes   forces himself into a woman   writes *there was no language*   for this dark ode

school was the bloody gash of sifting   my brown 300 lb frame   through pale mesh   I joined crew

we scrimmaged on American Lake   I waited cold starboard   dropped oar to blue   I rowed

I can remember the two times I've made white men cry   I was 19 on a doorstep   26 in a boardroom

the easiest way toward white sobs   is the precision of a Black woman breaking down   what she's owed

I almost killed my father three times   in the space of an hour   finally, he yelled

slower, Candace   you're too early for your date   with death   (I never slowed)

THE DARK DIARY

I lost / astonishment
absconded from / the glamour

of youth's futile / wanderings
life hadn't been worth / a day's breath

I need the greatest / possible risk
a pure unpractical / spirit

a sort of eager fatalism / I am the most
dangerous thing: a recollection / of night   (of love, too)

a blazing Dark / so extraordinary
there was nothing / on earth

to prevent me / killing
who I pleased / his consciousness

silent ruin / his mask heavy
like the closed door of / a prison

an unapproachable silence / evidently appetite
got the better / of him

I heard he was lying / helpless
in the sunshine / monologuing savagery: *life*

tries a man / I have a drop
of medicine / for a savage

like this / a mercy
a phantom / shining darkly

an image of death / carved by his glittering
mouth / he wanted to swallow

all: the air / the earth
all men / his deep voice

breathed long aspiration / white men hated the
Darkness which seems / to rise from

the ground / an intense Blackness
keeping uneasy vigil / of light's pure abstract

terror / sudden shock
sudden massacre / the possibility

of Blackness / beats the drum
of my Black heart / he rose pale

like a mist of vapour / he felt
the terror of position / of being knocked down

he cried / breathing horror
I blew / his candle out: moral

victory / paid by terror's
abominable satisfactions / I offered

my *Report* / *on the Suppression*
of Savage Customs: I know / the sun

is a vast manipulation / of light impulse
to conquer / Darkness at the colossal

scale of desire / in triumphant
Darkness / my anger

subsided / to a feeling of
infinite   (pity)

810   WHREN *v.* UNITED STATES

As a general matter, the decision

to stop a

black
motorist

is

valid

standardized procedure

we
uphold　　the constitutionality of a warrantless
search

only an undiscerning reader would

invalidate police conduct that is justifiable on the basis of
probable cause

in the *absence* of probable cause
simply explain　　the exemption from the need
for　　　　cause

officer
pretext

is

legal justification

We of
course agree   that the Constitution prohibits
selective enforcement of the law based on
          race   But

Subjective
intentions play no role in ordinary

motiva-
tions of   officers
good faith is the
touchstone of reasonableness

In-
stead of asking whether the individual officer had the proper
state of mind   ask
whether   it is plausible to
believe that

          f   e   a

                                        r

                                        is
                                        reasonable

the collective consciousness
of law enforcement

police manuals and standard procedures
provide

an objective means
of rooting out

serious misconduct

rare

exceptions not applicable here

police

discretion

outbalances   private interest
in avoiding police contact

officer

judgment

is

Affirmed.

A GOOD COP

This poem is an erasure and rearrangement of phrases from the New York Times Magazine's *police profile, "The Color of Suspicion," written by Jeffrey Goldberg in 1999.*

is a bull-
necked, highly
caffeinated drug
warrior

He can tell
if a man's lying
by the pulsing
of his carotid artery

A good cop is born
to seize crack
Always looking for bad
guys. The back

of his neck is burnt
by the sun
He can smell
crack cocaine inside

a closed automobile
He is a walking
polygraph machine
A good cop kills

before he is killed
smells the burning
marijuana
predicts the black will

resist. A good
cop pulls the car
over for speeding
Knows the art

of pretext. Good
cops speak of black
often: *A spitting
image. Death's*

*door. Black
black, black
black*. A good cop
does not think

of himself
as a racist. He believes
he is in possession
of a truth

polite society
is too cowardly
to accept.

BLACK, BODY

Antonin Scalia's WHREN v. UNITED STATES, 517 U.S. 806 (1996) opinion rearranged in order of word frequency, after Franny Choi

black body citizens civil equal fear freedom good guarantees guise inconsistent inconvenient incriminating Justice light marijuana ship wiretap writ youthful compliance race race traditional traditional respect respect faith faith faith opinion opinion opinion plainclothes plainclothes plainclothes valid valid validity illegal illegal illegal illegal occupants occupants occupants occupants right right right right sped speed speed speeding unmarked unmarked unmarked unmarked view view viewed views constitutional constitutional constitutional constitutionality constitutionality drug drug drug drugs drugs followed followed following following following id id id id id interest interest interests interests interests inventory inventory inventory inventory inventory inventory motivations motivations motive motive motive safety safety safety safety safety warrant warrant warrant warrantless warrantless evidence evidence evidence evidence evidence evidence investigating investigation investigation investigation investigation investigatory issue issue issue issue issue issued purpose purpose purpose purpose purpose purposes fact fact fact fact fact facts facts standard standard standard standard standard standard standard intent intent intent intent intent intention intentionally intentions invalid invalid invalid invalidate invalidate invalidate invalidates invalidation mean meaning means means means means means means order order order order ordinarily ordinary ordinary ordinary objective objective objective objective objective objective objectively objectively arrest arrest arrest arrest arrest arrest arrest arrestee arrested vehicle vehicle vehicle vehicle vehicle vehicle vehicle vehicles vehicles seizure seizure seizure seizure seizure seizure seizure seizures seizures seizures justifiable justifiable justification justification justification justified justifies justifies justify justify subjective subjective subjective subjective subjective subjective Subjective subjective subjectively subjectivity court court court court court court court court court court STATES States States States States States States States States States individual individual individual individual individual individual individual individual's individualized individuals individuals Fourth Fourth Fourth Fourth Fourth Fourth Fourth Fourth Fourth Fourth Fourth Fourth other other other other other other other other other others otherwise otherwise

See See See See see see see see see see See See law law law law law law law law lawful lawful lawfulness laws laws laws laws based based based based based based based based based bases basis basis basis basis basis basis pretext pretext pretext pretext pretext pretext pretext pretext pretext pretext pretext pretext pretext's pretexts pretextual pretextual pretextual violated violated violated violating violating violation violation violation violation violation violation violation violation violation violations violations violations reason reason reasons reasons reasons reasonable reasonable reasonable reasonable reasonable reasonable reasonable reasonable reasonable reasonableness reasonableness reasonableness reasonableness reasonably probable search search search search search search search search search search search search search search search searches searches searches searches searches stop stop stop stop stop stop stop stop stop stop stop stop stop stop stop stop stop stop stop stop stop stop stop stop stop we We We We We we We We We We we we we we we we we we we we we we we we we we we we officer Officer officer officer Officer officer officer Officer officer officer officer officer officer officer officer officer officer officer officer Officer officer's officer's officer's officer's officer's officers officers officers officers officers police police police police police police police police Police Police Police police police police police police police police police police police police police police police police police police police police

SPELLS FOR BLACK WIZARDS

Study finds white men who endorse racial 'color blindness' are less attracted to Black women

Pick poppies in a summer-lit field
On sight of a blood moon utter the incantation
"I don't see race"
in four dead languages
For a moonrise, your melanin
will be imperceptible

Baltimore County Council rejects housing anti-discrimination bill

Twist the corkscrew counterclockwise to open a bottle
of wine vinted the day you were born
Dab a drop of wine on your wrist
for each point of your credit score over 500
Imbibe a full glass for each year
of grad school you've completed
Your rental or mortgage application will fall
under gentler eyes

Tiny South Carolina town bans sagging pants, threatens fines

If 33 belts keep your pants pulled high
you won't be stopped or frisked
Breathe easy if the belts are all a different shade of blue
the hands of boys in blue
can't encircle your neck

White doctors may think Blacks have greater tolerance for pain

Wet your fingertip and point toward the breeze
If the wind blows east in the eve of your pain
ask your godmother to massage
her tears into your temples
Open your bedroom door with your left hand and carry a vial
of last night's sweat in your left pocket
Pangs of pain will inflame
your doctor's heart

Trayvon Martin was suspended three times from school

Your master's degree paid off in full
before a full compounding period
can stop blood
from escaping a wound
Honor it
with stillness and wine
at your altar

VOWS FOR A HERRING COVE WEDDING AMONGST LOVES AND PLOVERS

For Laimah Osman

You find my shirt ironed and tucked in today
I am the ghazal finding its radif today

Shakespeare misspoke when he said *love alters not*
Forgive me, I must alter him on the altar today

True love is alteration, is a pinking shear
A single loose thread will not undo us today

How did two displaced queers find home in each other?
Cupid's algorithm bowed his arrow that day

And dear Candace when did you know you'd found love?
Love is not found—love is the weaving we do each day

PANTHER GETS LOOSE

Gnaws His Way from Cage

Keepers with Net, Ropes, and Chain

---

        spread terror
                         in the neigh-
borhood for miles around.
              a hunting party

                         platoons
of police from three police stations

     doing whatever mischief

  The panther is a young male,
             is a fine specimen of the
    tribe, being eighteen

              Folks

                   could hardly be-
lieve an animal could be so active.

                    The hand-
some brownish   fellow

had evinced desire for freedom at times,
  had never made any wild breaks

had seen captivity all
its days.
There had been no thought of the pan-
ther's teeth in the building of the prison,

shouts of laughter, joking, mer-
riment and carelessness suddenly changed
into fear and dread when

The panther

liberated himself

NOTES

"The Dark Diary"

This poem is an erasure of Joseph Conrad's *Heart of Darkness* and *The Congo Diary*.

"John Henry Suffering and Dying in the Arms of His Polly Ann After a Ventricular Rupture Resulting from Overwork"

While writing this poem, I read the scholarship of Dr. John Garst. In his book *John Henry and His People: The Historical Origin and Lore of America's Great Folk Ballad*, Dr. Garst argues that the events in the "Ballad of John Henry" take place in Alabama along the Coosa Mountain Tunnel. In the poem, I borrow a phrase from Robert Hayden's poem "Middle Passage."

"Fruit"

This poem borrows lines from Abel Meeropol's famous anti-lynching poem "Strange Fruit."

"Crown Heights"

One day in 2016, I saw that the New York Public Library had developed a new website called OldNYC. On the site, you can find your address and see an archival photo at that exact spot. When I clicked on the intersection of Crown Street and Nostrand Avenue, I was shocked to see a castle-like penitentiary. That photo inspired me to read archival issues of the *New York Times* and the *Brooklyn Eagle*. The Brooklyn Public Library's article titled "Crow Hill Castle" was particularly informative.

"When I was 12"

Scientists have begun to link the concepts of intergenerational trauma and epigenetics. I read the New Scientist article "Fear of a smell can be passed down several generations" (2013).

According to the diaries of John Winthrop, *Desire* was one of the first ships to transport enslaved people to and from New England. In 1637, the ship transported 17 enslaved indigenous people from Massachusetts to Bermuda. *Desire* returned to the colony in 1638, carrying enslaved African people, cotton, and tobacco. I accessed John Winthrop's diaries on the website of the Marblehead Museum.

"Lady"

This poem is a whiteout erasure of the newspaper article "GHOST LADY TROUBLES BROOKLYN NEGROES" published by the *New York Times* on April 8, 1907.

"Bop for the Boys Scrimmaging in Prospect Park"

The bop is a poetry form invented by Afaa M. Weaver. In the first session of his Cave Canem workshop about the form, he encouraged me to think about music that really speaks to me. I use lyrics from the spiritual "Stay in the field, O Warrior!" as the refrain.

"Bop for a Black Man Caged in the Congo and the Bronx"

This poem is the second bop I wrote during Afaa M. Weaver's Cave Canem workshop. After coming across multiple articles about Ota Benga in the *New York Times* archive, I consulted *Spectacle: The Astonishing Life of Ota Benga* by Pamela Newkirk (2013). Like "Bop for the Boys Scrimmaging in Prospect Park," this poem uses spirituals in its refrain. I listened to recordings of The Davis Sisters singing "I Believe I'll Go Back Home" and Kathleen Battle and Jessye Norman singing "I Believe I'll Go Back Home / Lordy, Won't You Help Me" at the Metropolitan Opera.

"EXPLORER"

This poem is a whiteout erasure of the newspaper article "EXPLORER VERNER HOME WITH

AFRICAN CURIOS; Brings Mr. Otabenga, a Dwarf, to Act as His Valet" published by the *New York Times* on September 2, 1906.

"Quanta"

This poem alludes to the Heisenberg Uncertainty Principle.

"blackbody"

This poem was commissioned by Oye Group for a Summer Arts Festival with a climate change activism theme in Maria Hernandez Park. Many of the climate concepts in the poem were taught to me by artist-activists at Superhero Clubhouse. I use climate death statistics from Umair Irfan's *Scientific American* article "New York City Could See Thousands of Heat Deaths by 2080."

"Owed"

This poem uses a line written by Pablo Neruda (found in Adam Feinstein's *Pablo Neruda: A Passion for Life*).

"WHREN v. UNITED STATES"

This poem is a whiteout erasure of the 1996 United States Supreme Court decision that pretextual stops are not a violation of the Fourth Amendment of the Constitution of the United States of America. The unanimous opinion was authored by Justice Antonin Scalia and joined by Justices John P. Stevens, Sandra Day O'Connor, Anthony Kennedy, David Souter, Clarence Thomas, Ruth Bader Ginsburg, and Stephen Breyer, as well as Chief Justice William Rehnquist. This poem, alongside "A good cop" and "black, body" comprise a cycle of erasures commissioned by the Art for Justice program at the University of Arizona Poetry Center.

"Spells for Black Wizards"

This poem borrows news headlines from the *Baltimore Sun, RawStory, NBC News*, and the *Atlanta Journal-Constitution*.

"PANTHER GETS LOOSE"

This poem is an erasure of the newspaper article "PANTHER GETS LOOSE FROM THE BRONX ZOO" published by the *New York Times* in 1902. The poem was commissioned by the American Jewish Historical Society for visual artist Ido Michaeli's "Black Panther Got Loose From the Bronx Zoo" exhibition opening.

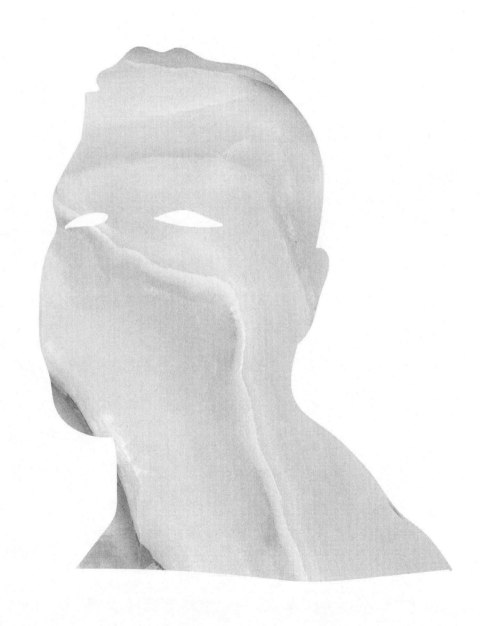

ACKNOWLEDGMENTS

My warm thanks to the editors and staffs of the following publications in which these poems first appeared (sometimes in earlier versions) for their generous support of this work: *Already Felt chapbook, The Atlas Review Chapbook Series, Bennington Review, Bettering American Poetry vol. 2* (Bettering Books), *Blueshift Journal, Brooklyn Poets Anthology* (Brooklyn Arts Press), Brooklyn Poets' *Poet of the Week, Copper Nickel, Cosmonauts Avenue, Day One, the Familiar Wild: On Dogs and Poetry* (Sundress Publications), *The Felt, Foglifter Journal, Foundry, Hyperallergic, Lambda Literary Review, Nepantla: An Anthology Dedicated to Queer Poets of Color* (Nightboat Books), *No, Dear,* the *PEN Poetry Series,* Poetry Project's *Poetry Canon, Prelude, Queer Nature: A Poetry Anthology* (Autumn House Press), *Redivider, The Rumpus, Sixth Finch, Soul Sister Revue: A Poetry Compilation* (Jamii Publishing), *The Slowdown* podcast, and *Wildness.*

I am grateful for the generous support received from Alice James Books, Brooklyn Poets, Cave Canem Foundation, Oye Group, Plexus Projects, and the University of Arizona Poetry Center.

RECENT TITLES FROM ALICE JAMES BOOKS

Burning Like Her Own Planet, Vandana Khanna

Standing in the Forest of Being Alive, Katie Farris

Feast, Ina Cariño

Decade of the Brain: Poems, Janine Joseph

American Treasure, Jill McDonough

We Borrowed Gentleness, J. Estanislao Lopez

Brother Sleep, Aldo Amparán

Sugar Work, Katie Marya

Museum of Objects Burned by the Souls in Purgatory, Jeffrey Thomson

Constellation Route, Matthew Olzmann

How to Not Be Afraid of Everything, Jane Wong

Brocken Spectre, Jacques J. Rancourt

No Ruined Stone, Shara McCallum

The Vault, Andrés Cerpa

White Campion, Donald Revell

Last Days, Tamiko Beyer

If This Is the Age We End Discovery, Rosebud Ben-Oni

Pretty Tripwire, Alessandra Lynch

Inheritance, Taylor Johnson

The Voice of Sheila Chandra, Kazim Ali

Arrow, Sumita Chakraborty

Country, Living, Ira Sadoff

Hot with the Bad Things, Lucia LoTempio

Witch, Philip Matthews

Neck of the Woods, Amy Woolard

Little Envelope of Earth Conditions, Cori A. Winrock

Aviva-No, Shimon Adaf, Translated by Yael Segalovitz

Half/Life: New & Selected Poems, Jeffrey Thomson

Odes to Lithium, Shira Erlichman

Here All Night, Jill McDonough

To the Wren: Collected & New Poems, Jane Mead

Angel Bones, Ilyse Kusnetz

Monsters I Have Been, Kenji C. Liu

Soft Science, Franny Choi

Alice James Books is committed to publishing books that matter. The press was founded in 1973 in Boston, Massachusetts to give women access to publishing. As a cooperative, authors performed the day-to-day undertakings of the press. The press continues to expand and grow from its formative roots, guided by its founding values of access, excellence, inclusivity, and collaboration in publishing. Its mission is to publish books that matter and preserve a place of belonging for poets who inspire us. AJB seeks to broaden our collective interpretation of what constitutes the American poetic voice and is dedicated to helping its artists achieve purposeful engagement with broad audiences and communities nationwide. The press was named for Alice James, sister to William and Henry, whose extraordinary gift for writing went unrecognized during her lifetime.

Designed by Tiani Kennedy

Printed by McNaughton & Gunn